Juggling

For Kids

Table of Contents

Introduction

Hey there, future juggler! Are you ready for an amazing journey filled with laughter, challenges, and some seriously awesome tricks? Well, you're in the right place because we're about to dive into the incredible world of juggling!

You might be wondering what in the world is juggling... Well, imagine tossing balls, beanbags, or even oranges up in the air and catching them in a fantastic dance of hands. That's juggling! It's like playing catch with yourself, and it's even cooler than it sounds.

But guess what? Juggling isn't just about tossing stuff in the air and crossing your fingers. Nope, it's way more than that! Juggling helps your brain grow big and strong, like a superhero's muscles. It boosts your hand-eye coordination, makes your brain super-smart, and even teaches you patience (yes, we'll need a lot of that for sure!).

In this book, we'll start with the basics and work our way up to juggling superstar. You'll learn how to juggle with one, two, and even three balls! Well, actually in this book we'll use beanbags, but you'll see me calling them balls a lot for simplicity. We'll have funny stories, lots of drawings, and tons of practice games and tips along the way to keep you entertained, and help you become the juggling master you were born to be.

Are you ready to jump into the world of flying beanbags and endless laughter? Let's do this!

Chapter 1 : Getting Started

Basic Juggling: It's All About Fun and Focus!

Hey there, future juggler! Before we dive into the world of juggling tricks, let's start with the basics. The first thing you may be wondering is, of course... what is juggling? And the next thing that will pop into your mind is... what do I need to juggle? Well, don't wonder anymore, here come the answers!

What Is Juggling?

Juggling is like a magical skill! Imagine you have three colorful beanbags (or balls, or whatever you like), and you toss them into the air, one after the other, catching them one by one without dropping any. But not only that, you can also move your hands while the beanbags fly through the air to do different tricks, like a dance with your hands! That's juggling! It looks like magic, but it's all about practice and patience.

Materials You Need

To start your juggling adventure, you'll need something to juggle with. You can juggle a lot of different things to add excitement and challenge to your juggling practice! Here are some fun items you can try:

- **Scarves**: These float gently through the air, making them perfect for beginners.

- **Beanbags**: The best option for beginners, they're easy to catch.

- **Balls**: Tennis balls and rubber balls work well.

- **Rings**: Juggling rings have a different feel and can create interesting patterns.

- **Fruit**: Try juggling small fruits like apples, oranges, or even lemons (be careful not to drop and squish them!).

- **Plastic cups**: You can stack and juggle them, it's a unique challenge!

- **Socks**: Grab a couple of rolled-up socks for a fun indoor juggling option.

- **Balloon animals**: If you have balloon animals, try juggling them for a whimsical twist. Regular balloons work too, give them a try!

- **Soft toys**: Juggle plush toys or stuffed animals for a cuddly experience.

- **Glow-in-the-dark objects**: You can try these for a nighttime juggling show.

Remember, safety first, so start with objects that won't break easily or you can't hurt yourself with, and gradually work your way up to more challenging things. You can have a blast exploring new objects to juggle!

Anyways, while you can use balls or even oranges, we're going to focus on the superhero of juggling: beanbags! Why? Because they're the perfect sidekicks for kids and beginners, and now we're going to learn exactly why.

Advantages of Beanbags for Juggling

If you're wondering why beanbags make such a good choice for beginner jugglers, here are the main reasons: it's all about keeping things safe and easy!

- **Soft landing**: Beanbags are soft and squishy, that means that if you hit your head with them (it happens to the best of us!) it won't hurt a bit, or if you hit something around the house it most likely won't break.

- **Easy to catch**: Beanbags are super easy to grab because they're not round like balls, and they fit perfectly in your hands.

- **Stay put**: Unlike rolling balls or wobbly oranges, beanbags are less likely to roll. You won't have to chase them as they roll away!

- **Bright and fun**: Beanbags come in all sorts of colors, making juggling even more exciting and colorful. Plus, who doesn't love colorful beanbags?

So, with your trusty beanbags by your side, get ready to learn some amazing one, two, and three beanbag tricks that will make you the coolest juggler in town!

Chapter 2 : One Ball Wonder

Tossing and Catching One Ball

Okay, let's start with the basics! Tossing and catching one ball (or one beanbag) is like learning to ride a bicycle with training wheels. It helps us get used to the rhythm of juggling, and learn to move our hands in the right way. It's this easy: toss the beanbag from one hand to the other, making the shape of a rainbow in the air, and catch it with the other hand. Keep practicing, and soon you'll be ready to add more beanbags and learn even cooler tricks!

But first, here are some fun ways to get started with tossing and catching one ball, perfect for juggling apprentices:

- Up-and-Down Elevator.

- Magical Bounce.

- Zig-zag Dance.

- Catch-Me-if-You-Can Race.

- Friendly Handoff.

Those are some pretty cool names, right? Don't worry, now we're going to see step by step what you have to do in each of those tricks. Go grab your beanbag, we're about to start this juggling adventure!

Trick #1: Up-and-Down Elevator - The Juggling Express!

Imagine you're in a super cool elevator, like one from your favorite adventure movie. Hold your magical beanbag in one hand, and press the "up" button!

1. Hold your beanbag in one of your hands.

2. Toss the beanbag gently up into the air – it's going up to the next floor!

3. Watch it as it starts coming back down.

4. Catch it with the same hand, like a ninja catching a flying star!

It's like taking a fun elevator ride up and down with your beanbag buddy. Keep pressing the "up" button and catching it as it returns. Ding!

Trick #2: Magical Bounce - Beanbag Bouncing Bonanza!

Beanbags usually don't bounce, so for this trick you need a beanbag filled with rubber beans, so it can bounce back to your hand, it will amaze your friends or family because they won't expect it to do that. You can use a bouncy ball to practice as much as you want. Ready for some beanbag magic?

1. Hold your beanbag like it's the most special bouncing ball in the world.

2. Now, give it a gentle toss down to the ground.

3. Watch in amazement as it bounces up like it's got springs for legs!

4. As it bounces back up, reach out and catch it with the same hand.

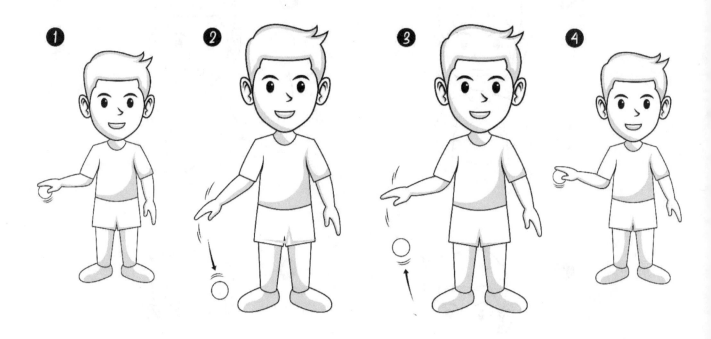

It's like playing a game with a super bouncy friend. Keep making it bounce and catching it like a pro magician!

Trick #3: Zig-zag Dance - Dancing with Your Beanbag!

Time to dance with your beanbag! Imagine there's a zig-zag line on the ground, you can even draw it if you're allowed to draw in your backyard or on the sidewalk. Stand in one spot, now you just have to follow the zig-zag path while tossing your beanbag.

1. Hold your beanbag with one hand, let's say the left one.

2. Step to the right with your right foot, following the zig-zag line. As you do that, gently toss the beanbag to the right as well.

3. Catch the beanbag with your right hand, while you move your left foot to the same spot as your right foot.

4. Now step to the left with your left foot, following the zig-zag line, as you throw the beanbag to the left.

5. Catch it with your left hand, while you move your right foot to the same spot as your left foot.

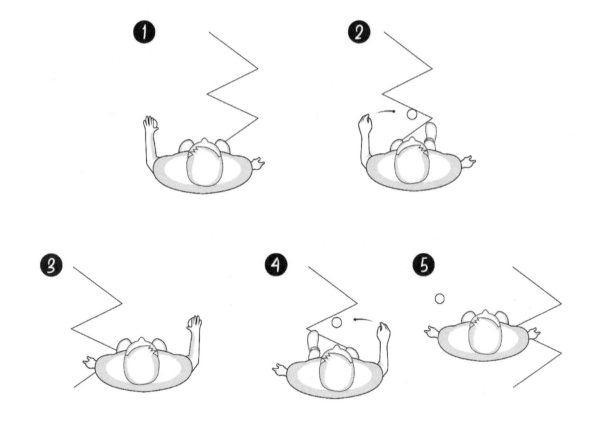

Keep moving and tossing your beanbag from side to side, like it's doing a fancy dance along the zig-zag line. You're the choreographer of this juggling dance!

Trick #4: Catch-Me-if-You-Can Race - Tag Time!

Get your running shoes on because it's time for a race with your speedy beanbag!

1. Hold it in your hand...

2. ...and give it a gentle toss forward.

3. Now, here's the fun part: start running, hopping, or even skipping to catch up with your beanbag before it lands!

When you catch it, give it another toss and keep racing. It's like playing tag with your beanbag, catch it if you can! Feel the thrill of the chase!

Trick #5: Friendly Handoff - Pass the Treasure!

Imagine you're passing a super special treasure between your hands, don't let it fall!

1. Hold your beanbag in one hand.

2. Give it a gentle toss to your other hand.

3. Catch it with your other hand.

4. Now, it's your other hand's turn to pass it back.

Toss it back and forth like you're having a friendly conversation. Your hands are the best of pals, sharing the beanbag treasure. Keep passing the fun left and right!

You're doing an awesome job! These tricks are just the beginning of this juggling adventure. Practice them with your beanbag buddy, and soon you'll be ready to learn even more exciting tricks!

Juggling Mistakes : How to Giggle Your Way through Them!

Juggling is all about fun and laughter, so don't worry if you make some juggling oopsies along the way. This book will also help you giggle through those mistakes and keep your juggling adventure full of smiles!

You don't believe me? Check out some of my most memorable oopsies! There's even an avalanche...

Oops #1 : Beanbag Avalanche

Sometimes, it might feel like your beanbags are falling from the sky like raindrops. Don't panic! It's just a little beanbag shower. To avoid this, make sure your tosses are gentle, not like trying to launch a rocket to the moon.

And if you do have a beanbag avalanche, just laugh it off and start again. It's like a beanbag party in the air!

Oops #2 : Beanbag Bumper Car

Ever had your beanbags bump into each other like cars in bumper car madness? It happens to the best of jugglers! To avoid this, try tossing each beanbag a bit higher so they have more space to dance.

If they bump into each other, give them a funny name like "Beanbag Bumpkins" and keep going!

Be careful to juggle them away from breakable things, just in case they bump into each other, and hit something else.

Oops #3 : Beanbag Escape Artist

Uh-oh, one of your beanbags decided to escape and roll away... It's like a little adventure for it! To avoid this, make sure you toss your beanbags straight up, not like trying to throw a frisbee.

If one escapes, give it a name like "Explorer Beanbag" and go on a hunt to catch it. It's like a beanbag hide-and-seek game! Just be sure to ask an adult for help if your beanbags roll under heavy furniture or dangerous places. The most important thing is to be safe!

Oops #4 : Beanbag Boomerang

Ever tossed a beanbag and it comes back faster than you expected? It's like a boomerang! To avoid this, practice your tosses with just the right amount of power, not like trying to launch a spaceship. If a beanbag surprises you, just laugh and say, "Nice try, beanbag!."

Oops #5 : Beanbag Crash Landing

Oops, sometimes a beanbag decides to make a sudden crash landing. To avoid this, focus on catching your beanbags gently, not like trying to catch a falling meteor.

If a beanbag crash-lands, pretend it's doing a superhero stunt and give it a round of applause. It's like a beanbag action movie!

Remember, mistakes are just funny detours on your juggling journey. Embrace them, giggle your way through, and keep practicing. You're becoming a juggling superstar one laugh at a time!

Juggling Journey : Level One - Mastering the Single Ball!

Hey, juggler! Before you dive into the world of two-ball juggling, let's have a blast mastering the single ball. These fun exercises will make sure you're all set to rock and roll with two balls later on. Get ready to level up your juggling skills right at home!

Game #1 : Juggle & Count Challenge

Turn your juggling practice into a math adventure! Toss your beanbag into the air and count how many times you can catch it before it touches the ground. Can you beat your own record each time? It's like a math game and juggling rolled into one!

Game #2 : Beanbag Toss & Catch Relay

Grab a buddy, like a sibling, parent, or a friend. Stand across from each other in your juggling space. Toss the beanbag to your buddy, and ask them to toss it back to you. Keep the toss-and-catch game going without letting it fall. Challenge yourselves to see how many times you can pass the beanbag back and forth without dropping it. It's a friendly juggling game of catch!

Game #3 : Around the World Challenge

Pretend you're on a juggling adventure around the world, visiting different countries with your beanbag.

Start by tossing it up and catching it with your right hand. Then, switch to your left hand. Keep going back and forth, like you're jet-setting with your beanbag buddy.

You can even make up stories about the places you "visit." Get ready for a global juggling adventure!

Game #4 : Juggle with a Twist

This one's all about adding a twist, literally! As you toss your beanbag into the air, give your body a gentle twist to the left or right. It's like you're doing a beanbag dance move. Catch it and twist the other way for the next toss.

Keep twisting and turning like a ballerina. Your beanbag is your dancing partner!

Game #5 : Juggling Jam Session

Turn on your favorite music and create a juggling jam session! Toss your beanbag in time with the music. Try to match the rhythm: slow for slow songs, and fast for energetic tunes. You can even add some dance moves while you juggle. It's like having a beanbag dance party in your own living room!

These fun exercises will make you a one-ball juggling superstar in no time. Keep practicing, and remember, juggling is all about having a great time! When you're ready, grab another beanbag, and go to the next chapter!

Chapter 3 : Double Trouble

Double the Fun: Adding a Second Ball!

Now, let's double the fun by adding a second ball to the mix! Are you ready to take your juggling skills up a notch? In this chapter, you're diving into the world of two balls!

Up until now, you've been rocking it with one ball, but get ready to impress your friends and family with some awesome tricks using two balls. It might seem a bit tricky at first, but don't worry, I'll explain everything step by step. With practice and a bit of patience, you'll soon be juggling like you were born doing it!

Grab your beanbags, and let's jump into the double-ball adventure! Get ready for some cool moves and tons of fun with these amazing tricks:

- Classic Cascade.

- Criss-Cross.

- Underhand Toss.

- Overhand Toss.

- Columns.

Remember, juggling takes practice, so don't worry if you drop the beanbags at first. Just keep trying, have fun, and soon you'll be a juggling pro!

Trick #1: Classic Cascade - Start with the Basics!

Are you ready to learn some awesome juggling tricks? Let's begin with the Classic Cascade, it's like the ABCs of juggling! The Classic Cascade is one of the basic tricks in juggling, and can be done with any number of things (although three or another odd number of balls are usually used).

You just have to throw each beanbag at an angle from one hand to the other in an alternating rhythm so that they don't bump into each other. All you have to do is follow these steps:

1. Hold one beanbag in each hand.

2. Toss the beanbag in your right hand up into the air, but slightly inward toward your left hand.

3. As soon as the first beanbag leaves your right hand, toss the beanbag in your left hand slightly inward, toward your right hand this time.

4. As the first beanbag starts to come down, catch it in your left hand.

5. Now, toss the beanbag in your left hand up into the air again, right on time to catch the second beanbag with your right hand.

6. Just like before, toss the second beanbag from your right hand toward your left hand. Keep repeating this back-and-forth pattern, and... you're juggling!

You're throwing a beanbag with your left hand, catching it with your right hand, and throwing it back to your left hand, and the same with the other beanbag (but the other way around). Just make sure one hand catches at the same time the other throws the ball, and you'll master this trick in no time!

Trick #2: Criss-Cross - Add Some Zig-Zags!

Ready to add a twist to your juggling adventure? Let's learn the Criss-Cross trick! Instead of tossing the beanbags to the other hand in an alternating rhythm, now you're going to toss them at the same time to make them cross like an X! This is all you have to do:

1. Begin with one beanbag in each hand.

2. Toss the beanbag from your right hand diagonally to your left hand. At the same time, toss the beanbag from your left hand diagonally to your right hand.

3. Watch them criss-cross like an X, and...

4. Catch the beanbags as they come down.

Repeat the whole process to keep criss-crossing them like a pair of dancing scissors. This trick may take a little more practice until you're able to catch both beanbags at the same time, but don't worry, you can do it!

Trick #3: Underhand Toss - Sneak Peek Below!

Time for something different, the Underhand Toss! Get ready to sneak a peek below the beanbags, here's the secret: you're going to toss one beanbag under the other! Just follow these simple steps:

1. Start with one beanbag in your right hand and one in your left hand.

2. Toss the beanbag in your right hand under your left hand. The beanbag will fall into your left hand from the outside, so to speak.

3. Now, toss the second beanbag in your left hand as usual toward your right hand.

4. Catch the first beanbag in your left hand, and the second one in your right hand.

Once you get used to doing this trick, you can go ahead and do it with both hands: first you throw the beanbag in your right hand below your left hand, and in the next move you throw the beanbag in your left hand below the right hand. Keep sneaking those beanbags under!

Trick #4: Overhand Toss - Over We Go!

Ready for an over-the-top adventure? This time, we're going over the top, let's learn the Overhand Toss! Ready? Here are the steps:

1. Hold one beanbag in each hand.

2. Toss the beanbag in your right hand as usual toward your left hand.

3. Now, toss the beanbag in your left hand over the first one. Instead of throwing it inward, move your hand slightly outward to give it more momentum.

4. Catch the first beanbag in your left hand, and the second beanbag in your right hand at the same time.

Once you get used to doing this trick, you can go ahead and do it with both hands as well: first you throw the beanbag in your right hand over the one in your left hand, and in the next move you throw the beanbag in your left hand over the one in your right hand. Keep those beanbags flying high over the rainbow!

Trick #5: Columns - Up, Up, and Away!

Get ready to build some colorful columns in the sky with the Columns trick! Imagine you're building two tall columns in the air at the same time, how high can you make them? It's as easy as following these steps:

1. Hold one beanbag in each hand.

2. Toss one beanbag straight up in the air, like you're sending it to the sky. At the same time, toss the other beanbag in your other hand straight up too.

3. Watch as they rise...

4. And fall back to your hands in two neat columns!

PRO TIP - Once you master the Columns, you can twist things and up the game by throwing and catching both beanbags with the same hand! Start with both beanbags in the same hand, throw the first one, and when it reaches the highest point and starts to fall, throw the second beanbag just in time to catch the first one. Just make sure to throw the beanbags slightly curved to one side, so they don't bump into each other while in the air, like this:

Keep those columns going up, up, and away! Remember, practice makes perfect, and it's okay to drop the beanbags. Just keep trying and have a blast on your juggling journey!

Juggling Fun with Two Balls - Let's Get Silly!

Now that we've doubled the fun with two balls, it's also time to get a little silly along the way. These exercises will make practicing juggling with two balls a lot of fun. Get ready to turn your juggling practice into a hilarious adventure!

Game #1 : School Pencil Challenge

Grab two pencils (if you don't have enough, you can ask your teacher if it's okay to borrow some). Pretend the pencils are your juggling beanbags. Now, start juggling with your pencils! It's like doing your schoolwork while having a juggling party. Can you keep those pencils spinning in the air to get a round of applause from your classmates?

Game #2 : Soccer Juggle Showdown

Are you a soccer fan? Pretend you're on the soccer field, and your two juggling beanbags are part of the game. Try juggling them while doing your best soccer moves. Kick your imaginary goals, celebrate with crazy dances, and make your stuffed animals the cheering crowd. Can it get any better than scoring goals while juggling? GOAL!

Game #3 : Plate Juggle Challenge

Visit the kitchen and ask for two paper plates. They're your juggling plates now! Decorate them with colorful drawings or funny faces. Juggle your plates like you're serving up laughter at a circus-themed restaurant. Invite your siblings or friends to join in and have a plate-passing party. But remember: serve only laughter on these plates, any real food could go flying everywhere!

Game #4 : Backyard Beach Ball Bash

If you have a beach ball, grab it! Pretend your beach ball is a huge juggling beanbag. You have a ton of options to give your juggling a twist with the beach ball: you can toss it back and forth with your hands while you juggle your two regular beanbags, you can juggle a regular beanbag and the beach ball, or you can juggle just beach balls if you happen to have two!

It's like having a beach party with your juggling buddy, don't forget to add some beachy dance moves and pretend you're surfing!

Beach balls can be quite large, so be sure to juggle with balls of a size you can handle to avoid damaging anything around you!

Game #5 : Juggling Twins Challenge

Find a buddy: a sibling, friend, or even a stuffed animal. Stand facing each other, and juggle your two beanbags back and forth. Wait... Can stuffed animals do that? Nevermind... Keep counting how many times you can pass the beanbags without dropping them. The person you can make the most passes with without dropping your beanbags wins the title of "Extraordinary Juggling Twin."

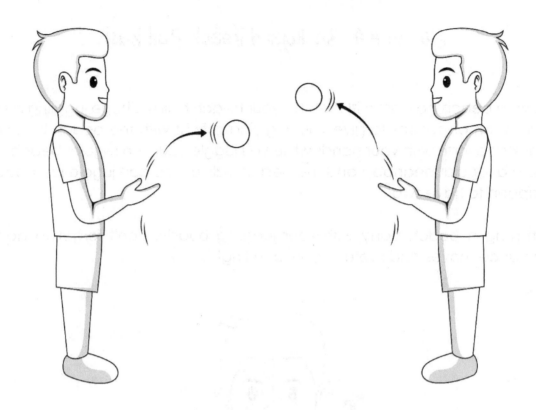

These silly exercises will turn your two-ball juggling practice into so much fun. Don't forget to laugh, make funny faces, and enjoy every moment of your juggling adventure. Juggling is all about having a fantastic time, and you're doing an amazing job!

Chapter 4: Three's a Charm

Three's a Party: Juggling with Three Balls

Are you ready for the next juggling adventure? Buckle up because in this chapter, we're adding a third ball into the mix. Tossing three beanbags might seem like a big challenge, but you're up for it!

Don't worry if it feels a little tricky at first. Just like everything else in the juggling world, practice is the secret. So, grab your beanbags, and let's jump into the world of three-ball juggling. Get ready for some jaw-dropping moves and loads of fun!

This chapter's bag is full of these amazing tricks just for you:

- Three-Ball Cascade.

- Shower.

- Tennis.

- Reverse Cascade.

- Mills Mess.

Remember, these tricks might take a bit of practice, so don't be discouraged if it doesn't work perfectly right away. Keep practicing, have fun, and soon you'll be a three-beanbag juggling superstar!

TIP - In the tricks you're about to learn you'll have to hold one beanbag in one hand and two beanbags in the other. You'll see that you'll always start with one beanbag in your left hand and two in your right hand, but that doesn't have to be the case all the time. Why? Well, because the most important thing here is that you're comfortable with the moves, so if you're left-handed you can start with just one beanbag in your right hand and use your left hand to hold the other two. Long story short: use your dominant hand to do the hard work and your non-dominant hand to assist.

Trick #1: Three-Ball Cascade - The Classic Juggling Dance!

You've mastered two-beanbag tricks, so it's time for a three-beanbag party! Let's start with the Three-Ball Cascade. Do you remember the Classic Cascade? I'm sure you can already do that trick with your eyes closed, so how about we add one more beanbag of fun? Let's do it! The steps you have to follow are quite similar:

1. Hold one beanbag in your left hand and two beanbags in your right hand.

2. Begin by tossing the first beanbag from your right hand up into the sky, but slightly inward toward your left hand (just like you do in a 2-ball Cascade). Be careful to hold the other beanbag in your right hand, it's not its turn yet!

3. Right after that, toss a second beanbag from your left hand, slightly inward toward your right hand this time.

4. Now, while those two are in the air, quickly toss the third beanbag from your right hand, slightly inward toward your left hand as well.

5. Catch the first beanbag that comes down with your left hand, and immediately toss it up again toward your right hand.

6. Catch the second beanbag with your right hand, and toss it again toward your left hand.

7. Then catch the third beanbag with your left hand, and toss it up again.

As you can see, all you have to do is keep tossing your beanbags from one hand to the other as soon as you catch them, you just have to move your hands a little faster than in the Classic Cascade. Catch and toss, catch and toss, catch and toss... Keep this juggling dance going, you're a superstar!

Trick #2: Shower - Beanbags Falling Like Raindrops!

Ready for a fun shower of beanbags? This trick is actually called the Shower, and it's like juggling under a waterfall! Only a few steps:

1. Hold one beanbag in your left hand and two beanbags in your right hand.

2. Start by tossing one of the beanbags in your right hand up really high.

3. While it's up there, toss the beanbag in your left hand directly to your right hand. At the same time, toss the second beanbag in your right hand up really high.

4. Quickly catch the first beanbag that comes down, and toss it to your right hand, right on time to catch the second beanbag, and repeat the same process.

TIP #1 - One way to get comfortable with this trick is to start small. What does that mean? Well, you can start with just two beanbags, one in each hand. Toss the beanbag from your right hand up high in the air, while tossing the beanbag from your left hand directly to your right hand. Do it slowly and, once you're comfortable tossing those two beanbags, speed up until you can do it fast enough to add a third one without running out of time to toss and catch it.

TIP #2 – There's another way to get comfortable with this trick by starting directly with three beanbags. How can you do it? Hold one beanbag in your left hand and two beanbags in your right hand. Throw both beanbags from your right hand high in the air, one right after the other, while throwing the beanbag from your left hand directly to your right hand. Then catch the first two beanbags with your left hand and start again.

Keep tossing one beanbag really high, and the next one really fast. It's like a beanbag shower, and the more you practice this trick, the more beanbags you can add! How many beanbags can you juggle at the same time?

Trick #3: Juggler's Tennis - Juggle Like a Tennis Pro!

Imagine that two of your beanbags are playing tennis using another beanbag! Does that make sense? It does now, it's the Juggler's Tennis trick, and it's a blast! This trick is a mix of the Classic Cascade and the Overhand Toss that you just learned a few pages ago, let's see it! Taking a few steps from here and there, this is what you have to do:

1. Hold one beanbag in your left hand and two beanbags in your right hand.

2. Start by tossing the first beanbag from your right hand up into the sky, but slightly inward toward your left hand (exactly the same as the Three-Ball Cascade).

3. Right after that, toss a second beanbag from your left hand, slightly inward toward your right hand this time.

4. Now, while those two are in the air, quickly toss the third beanbag from your right hand. Here's the twist: toss it toward your left hand as well, but slightly outward this time, like you're doing an Overhand Toss.

5. Catch the first beanbag that comes down with your left hand, and immediately toss it up again inward toward your right hand.

6. Catch the second beanbag with your right hand, and toss it again inward toward your left hand.

7. Then catch the third beanbag with your left hand, and toss it up outward again.

If you look at your beanbags, it looks like two of them are throwing the third beanbag at each other... They are professional tennis players!

Trick #4: Reverse Cascade - Juggle Backwards!

Get ready for a juggling adventure in reverse with the Reverse Cascade trick! Don't worry, you won't have to juggle upside down or with your hands behind your back or anything like that, you'll just have to throw your beanbags in a different way, look... These are the steps:

1. Hold one beanbag in your left hand and two beanbags in your right hand.

2. Begin by tossing the first beanbag from your right hand up into the sky, but slightly outward toward your left hand (just like an Overhand Toss).

3. Right after that, toss a second beanbag from your left hand, slightly outward toward your right hand this time.

4. Now, while those two are in the air, quickly toss the third beanbag from your right hand, slightly outward toward your left hand as well.

5. Catch the first beanbag that comes down with your left hand, and immediately toss it up again toward your right hand.

6. Catch the second beanbag with your right hand, and toss it again toward your left hand.

7. Then catch the third beanbag with your left hand, and toss it up again.

If you look closely, the only difference between the Reverse Cascade and the Three-Ball Cascade is that you toss the beanbags outward every time instead of inward. And if you look even closer, you'll see that the Reverse Cascade is the same as doing one Overhand Toss after another for all the beanbags. Keep the rhythm going: Overhand Toss, catch, Overhand Toss, catch, Overhand Toss, catch... You're a reverse juggling champion!

Trick #5: Three-Ball Columns - Columns with a Twist!

Do you remember the Columns? Throwing and catching two balls at the same time is never easy, but what happens if we add a third ball? That you will also be able to master it in no time, I am sure of it!

These are the steps to build columns like an architect:

1. Hold one beanbag in your left hand and two beanbags in your right hand.

2. Toss the beanbag from in your left hand, and one of the beanbags in your right hand straight up into the air. Now you have two balls going up in a straight line.

3. When those two beanbags reach their highest point and are about to start falling, toss the other beanbag in your right hand up in a straight line right in the center of the previous two.

4. Now, here's the tricky part: as the first two beanbags come back down, catch them with the hand they came from.

5. And finally, as the third beanbag comes back down, toss the first two beanbags straight up again, so you can also catch it with the hand it came from.

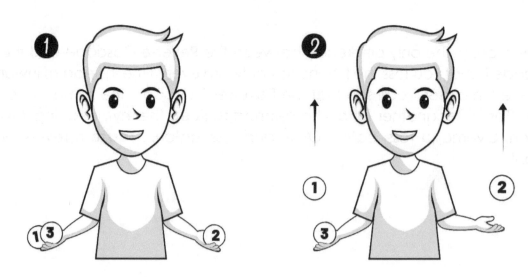

It might take a bit of practice, but once you get the hang of it, juggling in columns can look really cool! It's like making the balls dance up and down in a straight line. Keep practicing, and you'll be a juggling architect before you know it!

Practice these tricks, and you'll be the star of your very own juggling show in no time!

Triple the Fun: Juggling with Three Silly Balls!

It's time to kick your juggling skills up a notch, and add a bit of fun and silliness. These funny exercises will make practicing three-ball juggling your new favorite thing. Get ready for giggles and juggles!

Game #1: Soccer Juggle Showdown

Did you enjoy playing soccer while juggling two beanbags? I'm sure you did! Now, try juggling three of them while doing your best soccer moves. Kick your imaginary goals, and don't forget to celebrate with crazy dances!

Was there anything better than scoring goals while juggling two beanbags? Yes, juggling three!

Game #2: Juggle the Alphabet

Choose a letter from the alphabet. Juggle your three beanbags, and with each throw, say a word that starts with the chosen letter. Try to go through the entire alphabet without dropping the balls. This game will help you improve your juggling rhythm, and also your creativity. Think fast!

You can add a twist to this game to make it even more fun by choosing themed words, such as just words related to school, sports, or a season or holiday.

Game #3: Family Comedy Act

Gather your family members (or a few friends) and stand in a circle. Pass three juggling balls or beanbags around in a clockwise direction while juggling them! Everyone takes a turn tossing and catching. If someone drops a ball, they have to do a silly dance move. Now you have your own family circus!

You can always give the beanbags to the person next to you in the same direction, either clockwise or counterclockwise, or you can add a twist and let everyone choose which way to give them without prior notice. Everyone pay attention, you don't know who will have to juggle the beanbags next! Did you just juggle them? Well... it's your turn again!

Game #4: Juggling Countdown

Set a timer for a specific amount of time (e.g., 30 seconds or 1 minute, don't choose too long because your arms may get tired). Start juggling your three beanbags, and see how many successful tricks you can complete before the timer goes off. Challenge yourself to beat your previous record with each attempt. Can you do all the tricks you just learned in less than a minute?

Game #5: Supermarket Shopping Spectacle

Get three soft objects, like small plush toys or rolled-up socks. Pretend you're at a supermarket, and your items are the groceries. Juggle them while walking "down the aisle" (you can use a hallway or room). If you drop one, pretend it's an item that fell off the shelf. You might even make up funny grocery list names like "Giggle Juice" and "Laughter Loaf." Let's go on a hilarious supermarket juggling spree!

These exercises will turn your three-ball juggling practice into a super fun show. Laugh, be goofy, and enjoy every moment of your juggling adventure. Remember, juggling is all about having a fantastic time, and you're doing great!

Chapter 5: Tips, Games, and Challenges
Tips and Tricks to Boost Your Juggling Superpowers!

Now that you have mastered the basics of juggling and can juggle one, two, and three balls even with your eyes closed, it's time to level up your juggling skills. Get ready for some tips and tricks that will make you the juggling superstar of your neighborhood!

- **The magic of practice**. Imagine juggling is like learning magic tricks. The more you practice, the more magical it becomes! Set aside some time each day to practice your juggling moves, even if it's just for a few minutes. Practice makes perfect, and you'll see improvement in no time.

- **Go slow-mo**. When you're learning new tricks, slow down! Toss those beanbags up high and give yourself more time to catch them. It's like catching slow-motion shooting stars. Once you've got it, you can speed up everything!

- **Keep your eyes on the prize**. Pretend your beanbags are your friends, pets, or favorite toys, and you don't want to lose sight of them. Keep your eyes on the beanbags as they fly through the air. It's like having a staring contest with them!

- **Follow the beanbag bounce**. If a beanbag escapes and falls, don't let it run away! Follow its bounce and try to catch it before it rolls too far. It's like playing beanbag tag, and you're "it"!

- **Mix up your moves**. Don't just stick to one trick, mix it up! Try doing different tricks in one juggling session. You can start with the 'Cascade', switch to the 'Shower', and then throw in a 'Tennis' move. Surprise yourself with your juggling menu!

- **Practice, practice, pajamas**. Why not practice in your pajamas? Juggling is super fun, so make it comfy! Put on your coziest pajamas and have a juggling pajama party. You'll be the comfiest juggler in town!

- **Use your noodle**. Your brain is like a super-smart noodle. Challenge it by learning new tricks or juggling patterns. You can even create your own juggling pattern. The noodle power is limitless!

- **Share the juggle love**. Juggling is even more fun when you share it. Teach your friends or family some tricks, it's like passing on your juggling skills to others!

- **Laugh at mistakes**. Remember, everyone drops a beanbag now and then. It's part of the juggling adventure! Instead of getting upset, laugh it off. It's like telling a beanbag joke, and everyone loves a good laugh!

- **Juggle everywhere**. Turn your world into a juggling playground. Juggle in the park, in the kitchen (watch out for the cookies!), or even in your backyard. Juggling can happen anywhere and everywhere.

Keep these tips and tricks in your juggling toolbox, and soon you'll be juggling like a true superstar! Go out there and amaze the world with your juggling awesomeness!

Juggling Fun-O-Rama: Unleash Your Inner Juggling Star!

Get ready for an adventure filled with games, challenges, and fun activities that'll keep you entertained while mastering one, two, and three ball juggling – and even more!

Activity #1: Juggling Scavenger Hunt

Create a list of items around your home and give yourself a challenge: juggle while finding those items! Toss one beanbag in the air, and as you catch it, try to pick up an item from your list. Can you collect all the items while keeping that beanbag in the air? It's a treasure hunt mixed with juggling awesomeness!

Activity #2: Double Trouble Race

Team up with a sibling or a friend, I'm afraid stuffed animals can't play this time. Stand across from each other and start juggling two balls each. Race to see who can complete a certain number of tosses and catches first. The winner gets to do a funny victory dance while juggling!

There's a lot you can add to this game to make it more fun and challenging. What if in addition to juggling, you walk in a zig-zag line while doing it? Other options are walking around the room like in an obstacle course or juggling with your eyes closed! Would you dare to do that?

Activity #3: Three-Ball Tower Challenge

Gather your building blocks, and try to stack them into a tower while juggling two or three beanbags. Before you start you can give yourself a challenge, like making a 20 story tower or doing 5 juggling tricks before dropping the beanbags or tumbling the tower down, anything you can think of! It's your juggling fortress of fun!

Activity #4: Juggle & Guess

Invite your friends or family to a guessing game. Juggle your beanbags, as many as you want, while they try to guess how many catches you can make without dropping. Keep track and see if anyone guesses right! The winner gets a juggling-themed prize, like a homemade juggling badge, so it will also be the perfect excuse to do some crafts, so much fun!

Activity #5: Juggling Show Spectacular

You've become a juggling superstar, so why not host a juggling show for your friends and family? Set up a mini-stage, make colorful juggling posters, and prepare a fantastic routine. Invite your audience, and amaze them with your juggling talents. Don't forget to take a bow at the end, you're a juggling sensation!

Remember: Safety First!

When I was learning to juggle, I was practicing with some colorful beanbags in my room. I threw one beanbag up high, and it went straight into my ceiling fan! Whizz, crash, boom! The beanbag exploded, and tiny beans went flying everywhere, like popcorn at the movies. I tried to clean it up, but those sneaky beans kept popping up for months! It was like they were playing hide-and-seek with me. So, remember, when you're learning to juggle, watch out for those tricky ceiling fans, or you might end up with a beanbag explosion and a never-ending bean hunt in your room!

Why am I telling you this? Well, first because it always makes me laugh when I remember that story and I wanted to share it with you, and then because while we're all about having a blast with juggling, it's super important to be safe. If you're trying activities or games that involve objects around the house, like stacking things or scavenger hunts, make sure to ask an adult for help and guidance. Being careful and aware of your surroundings is like your juggling safety net – it's always there to protect you!

Conclusion

Well, we've reached the end of our juggling adventure, and what a fantastic journey it's been! I hope you had an absolute blast learning how to juggle with one, two, and even three balls. You've shown incredible dedication, creativity, and a sense of humor that would make any clown proud!

But guess what? The juggling journey doesn't have to end here – in fact, this is just the beginning! You can keep practicing and getting better at juggling. With each toss and catch, you'll become even more amazing at this incredible skill. And who knows, the next circus superstar might just be reading this book!

You can challenge yourself by adding more balls, exploring new tricks, and even performing your own juggling shows for friends and family. Keep pushing your juggling limits and remember to always have fun along the way.

Juggling isn't just about tossing objects in the air – it's about building confidence, improving hand-eye coordination, and unleashing your inner creativity. It's a magical art form that you've already mastered, and the world is your stage!

So, keep those beanbags, balls, or whatever you choose to juggle flying high. Embrace the laughter, celebrate your successes, and don't be afraid to try new things. You're on your way to becoming a juggling legend, and your juggling adventure has only just begun!

Now, go out there and spread the joy of juggling like the true circus superstar you are!

Made in United States
Troutdale, OR
12/05/2024

25784444R00038